LAND BOUND

LAND BOUND

Kathleene West

COPPER CANYON PRESS   1978

Some of these poems appeared in *Assay, Calyx, Gilt Edge, Jawbone, Jeopardy, Northwest Passage, Poetry Northwest, Prairie Schooner, Lincoln Star, Silver Vain, Slackwater Review, Yakima, BACKBONE* (Seal Press), *NO WARNING* (Jawbone Press).
"Roundel on a Sonnet by Marilyn Hacker" is a Copper Canyon broadside.

Thanks to Centrum Foundation, Fort Worden State Park, where Copper Canyon is Press-in-Residence.

Copper Canyon Press
Box 271
Port Townsend, Wa. 98368

for my parents
Alfred and Irma Linnerson

Contents

STILL LIFE IN GENOA, NEBRASKA

A toe-scraper, skirt-clencher,
I sidled through childhood
while Mother answered for me.
"She's five. She loves to read.
She's Daddy's girl."
I studied my shoes
as if they were Compton's pictured encyclopedia
and turned to Volume C
to read about the cat that got my tongue
and nurtured it, pink and moist,
until I fled from the towers of shoulders and chin
to the willow by the creek
and ransomed the eggs abandoned by a broody hen
for my unbridled tongue.

Hollyhocks

I

Fighting the tomatoes and sweet corn for light,
those wayward flowers clustered in my mother's garden.
Too stately for weeds, too plentiful
to be cherished, they spread in tight bunches,
nodding over the clothesline, peering in the kitchen.
They stuck close to the house, renewed each year
in the same places, safe from the plow,
safe from rooting hogs.
If their seeds wind-scattered beyond the hen house,
they tumbled unsprouted. Nothing lived easily
among the fireweed, the goldenrod
and the sharp rows of milo.

II

I stripped the showy spikes
and arranged my floral booty on the grass.
A toothpick jammed through the stem,
and each flower became a grand lady
draped in cloth of burgundy or scarlet.
Headless, flat-chested as I,
they glided in cotillions and quadrilles,
given grace by my hands.
But when I heard my father's tractor
and saw him driving up the pasture lane,
I left them motionless, dumb,
to run to the big wooden gate
and swing it open for him.
The discarded ladies lolled on the grass,
their flounces wrinkling into torn petals.

III

As he drove through the gate I held,
he looked straight ahead, and I swung behind him,
my greeting overcome by the machine's noise.
Mother's face pressed against the window, distorted
by the glass, and I knew just how she stood:
leaning forward, on one foot, hands braced on the sink.
The tractor sputtered out its hold on my father
and I watched his leg clear the seat
and touch him to the earth.
His face was caked with the gray soil he cultivated,
matching the evening drab of the farmyard,
the gravel, the silo and the elms indistinguishable
by color. With the strangling gray of dusk,
the hollyhocks were dull as pigweeds,
each bloom a faded trumpet, without sound.

Nebraska Cotton

When cottonwood blooms,
the flowers stain in dark clusters
like goldenrod dipped in wine.
And petals curl into tight, fisty buds
that strain white and weak inside.

    I found the rusty skillet.
    I foraged for twigs and green fruit
    to keep my brother fed and fit.
    And Nicholas stretched
    in a hammock between two trees
    and dreamed through my cottonwood chants.

In summer,
the seeds drop from the wind-split pod
and glide under fuzzy parachutes.
The farm blooms white and soft,
the milkweed fades, pigeons lose feathers
and the cows are pale spots in the pasture.

    Arranging the cotton in my hair,
    I practiced shoulders stooped with age
    and wisdom. I chose white words for my brother,
    but Nicholas said
    the cottonwood was a messy tree.

Like others,
with color alone to meet October,
the cottonwood yellows, grows skeletal.
Brown leaves shudder to the ground.

From my window, I watch Nicholas
hunched under the spare tree.
The wind designs dry leaves around his feet
and rocks the hammock back and forth. Tomorrow
I will heave the skillet into the thin creek
and imagine again: meals, words and love.

Thinking Of Rain In The Dry Season

Those summers when the Skeedee ran dry,
and the corn burned white, and the dust sealed
my father's face from smiles,
Aunt Bakie drove out from Omaha after church.
It was almost as if it had rained.
She brought marshmallow peanuts,
jellied orange slices
and the Sunday funnies.

Her name was Amelia
but she'd always been Bakie.
I quizzed her for explanations, leaping
over her parcels and weaving around her
as if she were a May pole.
Perhaps she fell into the flour bin as a child.
Or was enchanted by a hungry witch
and forced to bake bread and strudel in a tower.
And the curse blighted the land
not to be lifted until she escaped.

My questions ignored, she opened the packages
and turned the steamy morning to a holiday.
Balancing rhinestone sunglasses over her bifocals,
Mother agreed they'd stop the glare in the hayfield.
She posed in the fireweeds by the windmill,
flinging her hands over her head.
Then she and Aunt Bakie snorted and nudged each other
like two horses in forbidden wheat.

I jammed my hands into my pockets
and kicked up the dust,
but Aunt Bakie tossed a scarf over my clipped hair,
and told me to lean over the water tank to see
my beauty. My reflection floated from me,
an uncertain mermaid swaying in the water.
I ripped the scarf from my head, waving it
like a standard, and ran
from the smell of moss and wet stones
to Mother and Aunt Bakie.
They stood on the hill beyond the house,
their faces flashing in the sun like two mirrors.

Not A Hunter

Not that he didn't believe in killing.
He put to death
the ruptured lamb, the pullet sliced
by the mower, the kitten trampled in the barn.
Most, he tried to save, he and Doc Cruise
and not just the money ones.
Doc drove three miles
when Westring's milk truck hit Rocky Marciano.
Three miles, he griped,
and nothing to be done for that old black dog
but go ahead and shoot him.

I'd watched Dad try to hit things with guns.
He'd crumple a steer with one club,
determine the right knife-sharpness
                         for a porker's throat
but beyond the feedlot,
I don't remember an animal that he brought home, shot.

Did he feel mean, looking down a gun barrel
at something unfenced?
What buried all those bullets
in earth and fence posts?
I didn't ask.
He'd send tin cans flying into the air,
but not a pigeon, the raccoon that raided the goslings
or a coyote.

Thanksgiving, 1955.
Unmarked by shells,
ring-necked pheasant roasted in the oven.
He told Mom not to tell
but he found it
tangled in the barley stubble and tumbleweeds.
He freed the legs, hugged the flapping wings
and wrung its neck.

And that Easter
I watched him catch a jackrabbit, circling
closer and closer
("That way, you hypnotize 'em.")
until he grabbed it, thumb and forefinger,
like a cat's mouth on a gopher.
I didn't have to blubber about Peter Cottontail.
He let it go.

Only once he aimed to miss.
The Hokanson Bros.' dog, a fat collie,
bounded in our pasture to nip and tease the cows,
pushing them to gallop and crash through fences
into the corn. Nothing runs like a cow
in a cornfield. No chase is worse.
This was a neighbor's dog, needed a scare,
so one morning
my father sighted well above the dog

high on the elm
cracked the gun into the air
and watched the collie thud on the grass
like Lassie playing dead.

The last time I saw the twenty-two
down from its hooks in the garage,
my sister's youngest, Johnny Gregory had it
playing soldier on the workshelf.
I've never seen Dad so calm.
"Course it ain't loaded," he said.
"But we ain't takin' no chances."
Like a policeman discouraging the man on the ledge
he strained his hands for the gun, promising cookies
and a ride on the tractor.
My sister bit her knuckles,
but Johnny's one of us by half.
He considered.
Made it an even trade.

Never did I fantasize flight
on wing of tanager or pterodactyl.
Once I tested the bliss of free fall,
a dive from the haystack,
a feedsack strapped to my back.
Limping, moaning, I couldn't explain to Mother
why I had no sense.

Stretched in the grass, staring skyward,
past the swoop of barn swallows,
their shrill dips and glides,
I watched them perch,
smug on the power lines,
their fat beaks preening.
I wanted to skim those wires like ice,
trusting in the routine of right, left, slide on
and on, bound to the stretch of the lines,
hooked to their currents,
edging as far as power extends.

The Dark, The Closet, The Augustana Lutheran Church

In the cloakroom, Joanie Flaherty taught Purgatory.
The Ouija board affirmed I'd be there,
serving out my chunk of eternity
                    in that Never-Never Land
with no Catholic kin to pray for me.
Now I lay me, a child insomniac,
down to sleep with groan and creak,
wind sound, music under my bed—
the mice scuffling on the banjo Uncle Ben once played.
In the closet—the ghosts of my grandparents,
the Hall of the Mountain King, the Inquisition,
the words of Joanie Flaherty turning and seething,
and I pray the lord, my soul,
these years I suffocate under quilts
to keep me safe and sweating.

If I die, I'll have punished them.
A specter, a cherubim, I'll attend the funeral.
Will the coffin sprout rosebuds?
Will Mary Silverberg gather us at the river
while they weep and vow
never to spank me again?
Will Richard Green regret leaping from stairwells
and palpitating my heart at Sunday School?
Or if, before I wake,
I'm made an orphan. Oh, the pity
and ice cream! The tears and butterscotch!

Past the row of lilacs, the mulberry tree,
over the crumbled sheep shed, down on my stomach
to wriggle under barbed wire like a commando,
                    and run,

run to the middle of the field, spring wheat
still green, just beginning to head.
My hands to the sky
like a referee translating a touchdown,
I shout Damn it! God damn it!
And then I pray the lord, I'm sorry
I didn't know you heard
and take my soul
with my lucky beans, the piece of fool's gold
from California, the stone that might be petrified wood
to the elm that's my age
and climb until I am higher
I see further
leader of cornfields, adviser to pastures,
I am right. I have won.

First Argument Against Marriage

The day before your wedding,
barefoot on bluegrass and clover,
you assured me I would not fail
as flower girl.
When we raced across the lawn,
I thought you let me win
but the honeybee you trod on
stung revenge in your foot,
gave me the race.

We gathered around your swollen sole
and I watched him flame a paring knife
with a kitchen match.
I stood before you, my body a chubby X,
the way I'd learned to hold back
the farm animals that tried
to gallop toward freedom.
"I won't! I won't let you!"

With sensible words and needle,
Mother rescued us all.
It took more probing her way
but she worked the stinger free
and next day you stood easily enough
on white feet, but in the wedding pose,
the way I frown over the basket
of wild roses, you'd think I was the one
that got stung.

Still Life In Genoa, Nebraska, 1937

Uncle Olaf's portrait
leans on the creped table
that holds the black coffin
that holds Uncle Olaf.

Bearded, dusty and stern,
the oval-framed ancestors
look down on the ferns and roses
that decorate Uncle Olaf.

Aunt Emma attached a sprig of flowers
to Uncle Olaf's portrait
and rubbed the glass shiny
over his nose.

Clutching her dustcloth,
she stands by the hired man
who is taking the photograph
of Uncle Olaf's coffin.

Cousin Selma will take home
the roses, the ferns and Aunt Emma.
The hired man will take Uncle Olaf
to Valley View.

In Memory Of Mrs. Gerber

I remember the gloss of the dresses
in peacock colors, the nylons with hearts
and butterflies flourishing up the seams, the hunks
of rhinestone bedecking wrist and ears.
Six feet tall in her patent spikes, she towered
above the study hall, the basketball team,
the coach, topping them all
with a triumphant frizz of cinnamon hair.

Splendid in satin and velveteen,
she confided to our class the glamour
of her feather boa. "Lana Lobell!" my mother sniffed
at the gaudy clothes, selected from that brassy
mail-order catalogue of frivolous apparel.
The town was used to neutral women
who tinted their hair beige or brown
to match their sensible plaids.

Mrs. Gerber stilled
our wriggling rows with her command for immaculate
calligraphy. We copied
the footnotes to *Julius Caesar,* the directions
in our grammars. A misplaced conjunction
in a diagram, a smear on the page,
would send us crumpling and tearing
to the wastebasket to begin again
on unmarred paper.
She sat for an hour on a tack
without feeling it. Who could challenge
that confidence of height, that surety of jaw?

Dad always said those out-of-town schoolteachers
drove like the devil.
Smug in black dresses,
Joanie Flaherty and I went to the funeral.
Sitting in the basement of the Monroe Methodist Church,
with the non-relation, we stared at a loudspeaker
or each other, our stomachs gurgling.
By the last hymn,
we shook with pent giggles.
Only by holding our breath
could we escape past the open coffin.
I couldn't look to see what she wore.

Afterwards, we cruised main street,
from Scotty's filling station
to the Catholic Church,
each U-turn executed the same,
clean and perfect.

For My Mother, Who Lives

Healthy and sane, she speaks of dying.
It's the regularity of the pension—a monthly reminder
that time passes, she's old.
Although staying alive's a good investment,
death sounds easy, less complex for her
than driving three gravelled miles to the Farmer Store
or keeping my father off his tractor.
The graveyard lot purchased,
("First come, first served," she says.)
Valley View offers room for six
but we are seven.

She's not forgotten our number
but is there someone she'd rather not
have decaying beside her?
The youngest by a decade, am I to scrounge
my own crypt? Or is it better
not to have a spot guaranteed?

In her sleep, Aunt Bakie and Granny Addie,
firm-skinned and alive, stand in her house
and try to coax her away.
"But I didn't want to go," she says.
"Wasn't that a funny dream?"
Too practical for premonition, she tells me stories:
the time they changed Amelia's name to Bakie,
sewing corn shucks on a dress for Halloween,
and how Granny Addie returned all those snapshots
before she died.

Listing possessions, wondering what's valuable,
she invites me to choose my inheritance.
I sift through her jewel box—
fifty years of accumulation
and gather my treasures.
A watch, a ring, Grandma Linnerson's comb—
whatever fits
in small corners in a suitcase.
There are other corners, unfilled.

I remember when she told me
marriage was like a play,
and we speculated which of my sisters acted the best.
That was before I left at intermission.
Each time I leave Nebraska, she holds my shoulders
and looks at my face as if she'll never see me again.
But there's less space between us
than the time I chanted in Ladies' Aid:
"I'm five and my mother is forty-five."

In grade school I bragged about ancestors—Jesse James
and the fellow who used to be in history books
for digging out of prison with a spoon.
I don't need those legends now.
She can tell me five children were too many,
and know I won't cringe, imagining myself unconceived.
We have a tradition of survival.
Surrendering it to me, she goes on.

Letter From Nebraska To The Youngest Daughter

Here on the farm it's a dry October,
trees beautiful, weather pleasant and warm
and dry. Only thing, the wheat seed just lies
in the dry dirt. A few sprouted and pushed through
but it's a thin stand.

Nick came over to pick the corn across the Skeedee.
Dad's share turned out
to be one load of wet corn.
The government calls this farm a Disaster Area,
and Dad figures their payment will be a disaster.
But the old soy beans came through.
So that's why we can get along.

I don't think I told you
about hurting my toe this August. Old news,
as it's all healed up now, but sore
for a whole week. I dropped
one of those fish bowl glass plant terrariums
and cut my number two toe.

My old eye doctor died last winter
and I worried about my eyes
but Mrs. McKillup told me about a new man
in Columbus, and I can see better now.

Your last poem needs some clarification.
We reserved a plot for you by our side
in Valley View. We didn't think
anyone would care for a spot,
and we just aren't the type to tell our kids
we have a plot for them.
We might make them mad. Oh yes,
and those unfilled corners of your suitcase
are really filled—filled with love.
It is hard for me to express it.

We are all well around here.
Dad sold the last of his cattle. Feels lost
without cattle to look at and feed.
But we still get about six eggs per day
from the old red hens. And I have my three cats
with more on the way by the looks of things.
Hope all is going
ok for you.
                    Love from
                    Dad & Mother

WIND, WOMAN AND MAN

"*Please do not smell the flowers.*
They have been sprayed."

In these memorial gardens, flowers aren't
for smelling. Mindful of breath,
we move toward the Locks and try
to sniff the salty difference between the Sound
and Lake Union. Most of our lunch
we fling to the gulls, bits of bread
that bloom between the sun and water, flashing
pink as blossoms. We are the children
who stuffed beans in their ears, listened
to the crone's advice to follow your nose.
Around us, the banned flower grows,
in the green-leaf water,
the gulls plunging after the bread
like late summer petals.

In Mother's bedroom, we sprinkled perfume
behind ears and knees, drew moist circles
around each wrist to create her smell
on our bodies. Do not smell the flowers,
drenched with age, sprayed with the essence
of the women you will become.
We do not understand their warning
and walk in the garden,
touching the rosebay with our fragrance.
Tonight, in our separate homes,
we plot gardens for our daughters
and write letters we will hold, undelivered,
for years. We have no warning,
only each other and the warm smell of love.

Landscape With Wind, Woman And Man

I

No wind in this city. Voices rise
straight as a smokestack, black columns
that jut into the sodden air,
and your breath rises
in short spurts from this page. Not sun
but wind. Need wind that whips blue shirts
into fat, decapitated torsos strung
on a line, wind like a sharp cornhusk
to slit your skin. Need wind.
The woman on the hill
calling down to the figure
hidden in the barn shadows
feels the wind blow her words
back to her throat.

II

From the two-fisted shade of the barn
a man steps,
feels the western sun grip his body
and stretch it long
like a lightning rod. He knows
the wind will carry his words
easily upward
to the woman willowing on the hill,
and smiles at the sinking light
that glitters the field between them.
Try to imagine how far
the sun pushes the line of her body
before the cut shadow
and the gleaming leaf
soften into one breezy gray.

III

Now the arranging.
Dusk. Sun and wind both
dying down. Bring the woman down
to the valley and advance the man
to the edge of the bleached corn rows.
Did you think I take the part
of the woman, and you the man?
Too much risk to write our breath
in broken lines. A fade-out.
Leave them in the smeared gray.

IV

I enjoy this. I want
to make opportunities for them,
want to move them like scissor steps.
And yet, I find
they have control
over me. They refuse to walk
toward the house or wander
in the cottonwoods. They hide their faces
from me. I must go to them,
but I am not allowed to pace in the valley
or keep vigil on the hill.
Now I understand.
The wind, the wind is for me.
I hover, dip and whirl,
bend the brome grass to their feet,
lift their hair and twirl it,
tangle it together
in the air,
the air I move.

Full Moon

Open and bold as a ghost
or moth
a man beneath the bright window
flutters his hands to beat on the pane

a voice challenges
harsh
female
he must reply
he scrapes something feeble
and useless from his throat
she can't hear
no one can hear
no one can see

a square of curtain drawn tight
across the window
breeze to push the material
and reveal a line of dark table
a full-blown rose releasing its petals
and listen
two women
distinct and exposed
as a voice

he concentrates on the curtain
blurs their words to no-sound
blurs their imagined bodies
to faint outlines
he cannot see
no one can see

but the hand that pulls the curtain
is large and inescapable as the moon
he is betrayed
rose petal drops to his angry skin
above that fat white hand
a face
he can see
nothing between
hand and face unmatched
the face
thin and long
as a scream

he rips the rose petal from his skin
like a scab
heaves it back to the hand
and runs
his conspicuous body
wrapped in the scream
like an ugly raincoat

Bones In The Womb

"As you do not know the way of the wind
or how the bones grow in the womb."
——*Ecclesiastes*

The leaves hang from the maple like sloths,
like dead sloths. I wish for a torrent
to strip them from the tree. Better the barren limbs,
a dignity, than these shoddy clumps,
remnants of a plump and glossy season.

I rage against the false warmth in my kitchen,
the thin stem of the passion plant teasing the window
with two buds. I cannot feed its appetite,
cannot wish for its flower. For me, a surface
slick and flat as the table, a thing growing
without promise of spring.

As a child I petitioned God for boots
to scuff through layers of leaves, the kick, crunch,
skip over dust. Now, after wishbones, early stars,
the search in clover, my protected feet skid
through leafmeal and glue sticky prints on my stairs.

I dream of stairs, hacked and splintered
from a slab of cottonwood. I could say
they lead nowhere, the cellar I recall
accessible only by leaping down, could say
I wake, sweaty, screaming for wind to grip my skin.

To My Twin Sister Who Died At Birth

Never did I learn to share. Expanding
the womb with my fat kicks, anticipating the rush
to the picnic table for home-frozen ice cream,
sneaking the wishbone from the Thanksgiving platter,
the unsuccessful nights flailing out
my portion of a bed, I cramped you, small
and thin. Now, pausing before a mottled rock
to chisel my daughter, I imagine
a woman who lives.

When Aunt Bakie brought the silver dollars,
you smiled and bounced.
I cried under the coffee table.
The same temper, the passion for chocolate,
but long after you've flared
and forgiven, I pout
and plot disasters
for Dr. Dalton and the allergy shots.
Never soap under the fingernails to stop
your nibbling! Never pacing the rug
for lack of a smoke!

From Mazatlán and lover, you send pieces
of the novel in progress, self-portrait
of a woman who loves easily and for years.
Mornings, I shiver a glance to the mirror
and wonder how you look,
but you won't leave the sun and I'm held
by the iron rays of the rain. Next month
a birthday. Did you live
to hear the slap, my howl?
I share it with you now.

Bitches Brew

"What good is it if you dazzle him with your
Shrimp Marengo, strike him dumb with your Rum Torte
and then disappoint him with a so-so cup of coffee?"
                    —*Farberware advertisement*

Shall I dazzle you?
Fling glowing casseroles around your head,
spread iridescent loaves of bread with fiery jam,
                              serve cake
with currants blinking like Christmas bulbs?
In this kitchen, where every appliance is a Sunbeam,
I will charge you with the power in my skin.

Sit at my table, ground yourself,
but do not try to speak.
The Swedish rye has paralyzed your throat.
Now that you are mute and choked
why do you force words?
How many times have we sat, imagining conversation,
each waiting for the other's mumble?

Prying your mouth open, you stammer sounds
that I care not to interpret.
You are blind and dumb in my house, frustrated
without sight or tongue. Rest
your anxiety. Smell the fragrance
                              of the steaming soup.
I've simmered bones for hours.

Your face grows numb, the heartbeat slows,
we're thrusting back in time, moving nineteen years
to Nebraska to stand in the snow and watch
for the northern lights. It's cold, so cold there
and the aurora is a frozen flare
          but when each breath slices a lung
and ice needles sting our feet,
we'll go inside the farmhouse—the door unlocked,
a basket of wood by the stove, and the coffee bubbling.

Welcome Home

He no longer walks with ease
in this house.
When he takes a corner, his heel
treads on the baseboard, his ankle
scrapes plaster. Last night
he stubbed each toe
in the painful distance between the light
and the edge of the bed.

She demonstrates her own awkwardness,
belly-flops in the pillow, tangles the sheets
in her twisting legs, but he rejects
this gawkiness.
She's no more clumsy than an eel.
He slicks her hair back
from her face, explores the perilous smoothness
of her cheek,
her neck.
Next day he slips
on the kitchen linoleum.
The black and white squares shimmer beneath him
like sweat.

In the dark he wakes often
and feels her curled tight
and stiff as a sculpture.
He tries to half-circle her,
to warm her chill body straight.
She complains of leg cramps
and jokes about growing old.

They do speak of love
and their words are crisp
and delicate. He remembers
the bright window of a pastry shop, rows
of Florentines, thin wafers repeating
their lacy pattern and scattered sugar
catching the sun like ice floes
chipped and slow
on a winter river.

What Maywell Said

for Mike Henderson

Maywell said we could wade the river.
We followed his lines,
the map crayoned on a bit of sack, drawing us
down the washed-out road to crash
through the forest. At the river we tumbled
down the bank and lined like subjects
at the edge. As the water sucked up to my waist,
I'd never felt so short. But Maywell said
we could wade the river.

In a midnight huddle, we stoked the fire
with tales of bears and Simple Gilbert,
the enormous Islander who amused himself
lumbering through campsites and peering
in tents. When the twigs snapped behind us,
we traded belief that these bears
were properly uncivilized, ignoring scraps
and humans. And Maywell said
Simple Gilbert hadn't been seen for years.

But we listened too hard
to the sounds around us. Ripping
a blade of grass from the ground,
you made it whistle. Between the obscene blasts
and our nervous giggles, you said
we ought to hear Maywell on a blade.
It whistled us to bed, curled us
claw-tight in our sleeping bags
and dreamed us close and dark as bears.

Bear and Maywell we saw the last day,
safely from the pickup for both, watching
the bear thrust snout to the wind
and twist back to the forest, watching
Maywell's car zigzag backwards
on the gravel, tacking from edge to edge
to stop, bumper-close, and line us
in his sight. Maywell said he'd see us again
and watched us down the road, the dust separating us
like a river too deep to wade.

Spin Web, Catch Prey, Suck Blood

for F. B.

Out from the green on the stream edge,
the spider hung over the log that forced
the water faster. You, in a squat,
an orange cup dipped in the creek, staring
at the spider like a volunteer following the sway
of the hypnotist's chain. The cup rose,
your wrist flicking it at the single thread.
Eight ounces poured on a spider—forty nights
of monsoon assaulting a village. Now a battle.
Atlas among arachnids, it clung
to its line. Another slosh, and it whirled
to keep its space in your vision. Your final cup
set eight legs flailing for broken silk, a leaf
and retreat. You nodded and rested
the cup on your knee. It's a matter
of timing, you said, not offending.
What's a spider to me?

And what were you to the spider?
That night, crouched by the fire, spinning
tales of Bigfoot, I watched daddy longlegs
escape from the smoulders and run
at you. Batting them away, you muttered
something about fire, spider and time.
The half-rhyme stuck in your throat
like a gnat made fast in a web.

We watch, intent, for a green spot
to replace the sun,
a reminder of bright, close circles.

But we look at black and violet—
the darkest island, the streak of cloud
that cracks the sky.

We are seven women arranged
on slabs of rock. If a ship slipped by,
which of us would beckon?

Cold air slides up to our elbows,
fits our summer skins
like a coat.

We leave with clear faces
before the dark makes us touch
to find one another.

On Hearing That My Sister Is Managing
A Minit Market In A Ski Resort

You have managed before. In '49
when the storm crashed a window in the schoolhouse,
you, teacher,
inches shorter than the boys hunkered at the stove,
knew it was stay and freeze
or push through the snow.

It was like circling a Monopoly board
to avoid Boardwalk or jail,
throw yourself in the wind, count each step
and hope the move ends on safe property.
Bobbing up and down like tokens,
the children pressed behind you.

In the family, you are the worrier.
Is that how it began—when you felt
the sickness surge through your stomach
with fifteen lives tied to you?
Through hot coffee and comforters
the uneasiness held,
lashing around you like a blizzard.

And now you work in a package of sculptured snow,
count cans and cartons,
no longer shut in the stun of frost on your face,
but still you push to stay awake,
tie yourself, like string, to this life.

The plants breathe and mass,
spiraling up the walls, creeping
on the chairs. Once, we shared fruit
in the kitchen and now an apple tree curls
its branches around the thyme and sage.
I don't know where its roots trace,
but in Becky's house, I am attached,
supported, I grow.

Dancing On Eggs, Notes Toward A Human Arrangement

They stand in a kitchen,
this man and this woman, everything white
around them—walls, cupboards
and the textured uneven floor. A slash of color
cuts from an open door, crumpled sheets
red and yellow. Opposite, a dark window
marks the determined vigil of this night.

Perhaps some dialogue. The woman complains
of pain in her womb, bleeding
before her time, and the man
responds somehow, in a manner
to be worked out later.
They each want to move.
But the floor will give beneath his foot
and spring up like rain forest moss.
This is what she wants, each step
effortless and bouncing as a heartbeat.
And he envies the obvious trail
she strings behind her.
So they stand, suspended
yet safe in their separate positions,
supported by a counter, an edge.

As the windowpane lightens, patterns of branches
and clinging winter leaves appear
on the stiff white of the walls.
Something outside makes the shadows
light on their faces.

Plan another scene,
in which they move toward each other,
not with arms outstretched
and a slow-motion canter
but in the stiff jerks
of adolescents unaccustomed
to synchronize an embrace.
Show the floor cracking and bursting beneath them
and when they meet by the spice rack
and touch hands, be sure
the handclasp is difficult,
the fingers slide apart
in slippery exchange
before they close and hold.

The Court Jester Interviews Her Successor

If you're comfortable in my choice of trappings,
you needn't invest in outfits.
The tunic's a shade brief, but a row of scallops
or thick fringe to mask the thigh disguises
all shortcomings, and motley's still expected
in this profession. A pom-pom's missing
from the right slipper. I lost it
falling head over heels one night.
No, please don't demonstrate your flips.
Proficiency is not required.
You like the cap? Not traditional,
but you have to watch your symbols these days
and a cock's comb . . . well, it betrays both my sex
and my pretensions, if you know what I mean.
I've always been fond of asses' ears,
but employers find them intellectually insulting.
Oh yes, that's still part of the job
but it's gamier now. Unveil the sarcasm,
pluck out the barb, find the needle
buried in your voice. What?
Too seriously? Yes, I suppose I did.
Worn out at 30, my bells rusted,
my tongue rusted.
But it's an easy job. Really, so little is expected.
It feels nice, doesn't it, to shake your head,
the tassels striking your cheek.
They're soft as Rapunzel's hair and just as strong.
The bauble. A passing pilgrim carved the head
in my likeness. You can alter it later,
but at first you may find it comforting
to have a head nodding beside you
that's not your own.

Note the sharp protruding tongue.
If you're in the habit of wandering alone,
late at night, you'll find it an excellent weapon.
It's like looking into a mirror
to stand across from you. Material?
Oh my dear, even we domestic buffoons have evolved.
A witty story or two and a rhythm—
Listen, grimace, comment. One, two, three.
Shake the bauble, sway the tassel, slipper spin
on velvet sole. One, two, three.
You're out.

Roundel On A Sonnet By Marilyn Hacker

We need more boozy women poets,
I read. The whiskey blurs, confuses
me near enough to accepting it,
but first—we need more booze.

And then, define the crucial word. To booze:
drinking to excess, and there we've set
the standard to join our Muse
of bourbon-in-hand women poets, reciting sonnets

in colorful bars, and not just sonnets,
but bawdy pantoums and tough lyrics—to lose
"poetess" forever, but Hell—we don't need more poets
of any kind. We need more booze.

Kathleene West grew up on a farm three miles west of Genoa, Nebraska. She lives in Port Townsend where she works as a printer's devil.

Sixty copies of this book were printed by Kathleene West on Nideggen paper from hand set Spectrum and Palatino types and bound in cloth over boards by Lincoln & Allen, Portland. One thousand copies were photo-offset from the letterpressed original.

The printing was made possible by an apprenticeship grant from the National Endowment for the Arts, a federal agency and the encouraging words of Sam Hamill & Tree Swenson.